Witness History Series

THE THIRD REICH

David Williamson

Wayland

Titles in this series

China since 1945
The Cold War
The Origins of the First World War
The Russian Revolution
South Africa since 1948
The Third Reich

Cover illustration: The frontispiece to the official Nazi
history book, *A New Germany*.

First published in 1988 by
Wayland (Publishers) Ltd
61 Western Road, Hove
East Sussex BN3 1JD, England

© Copyright 1989 Wayland (Publishers) Ltd

Editor: Catherine Ellis
Designer: Ross George
Consultant: Beryl Williams, Reader in modern European history
at the University of Sussex.

British Library Cataloguing in Publication Data
Williamson, D.G. (David Graham), *1940-*
    The Third Reich.
    1. Germany, 1919–1945
    I. Title   II. Series
    943.085

    ISBN 1–85210–321–3

Typeset by Kalligraphics Limited, Horley, Surrey
Printed and bound by Sagdos S.p.A., Milan

Contents

The Weimar Republic

THE WEIMAR REPUBLIC was formed as a direct consequence of German defeat in the First World War, followed by revolution. If the war had not been lost by October 1918 and Germany plunged into chaos by strikes and mutinies in the army and navy, it is difficult to see how the German nationalists, industrialists and generals would have ever accepted a democratic constitution. However, in November 1918 they had no choice but to bow to the storm. On 9 November a republic was declared and the Kaiser abdicated.

From the beginning the Republic failed to secure its position. It was supported by the Liberal parties, moderate socialists (the SPD) and the Catholic Party (in the centre). But it had to rely on units of the old Imperial army and on the newly formed Freikorps which were full of right-wing volunteers, who hated the Republic, to defend it from the Spartakists (communists). It failed also to sack the Kaiser's civil servants, judges and professors, who could not always be relied upon to support it.

In its early years the Republic faced so many problems that it had no chance of winning over its enemies. It was hated by the nationalists, who could not come to terms with Germany's defeat, and by the extreme socialists and communists, who believed that the Weimar Republic had betrayed the revolution. It also had to accept a dictated peace from the Allies as laid down in the Treaty of Versailles, which reduced Germany's army to 100,000, stripped Germany

■	Lost by Germany 1919
■	Demilitarised Rhineland 1919-1936
□	Austria-Hungary until 1918
■	Saar: League of Nations control 1919-35
■	Plebiscite areas
■	Former territory of Imperial Russia

Europe in 1919 after the Peace Treaties. Germany, with the collapse of Austria–Hungary and Russia's loss of her Western territories, was potentially the strongest state in Central Europe.

▲ This Democratic Party poster charts the obstacles the Republic had overcome since 1919.

of her colonies, gave West Prussia to Poland and handed over the Rhineland to an Allied occupation, which was to last for fifteen years. It also committed Germany to a crushing programme of reparations, which in May 1921 was finally fixed at 132 billion gold marks.

For the next four years the constantly changing governments of the Republic were too busy dealing with threats of putsches from both the Left and Right and with pressure from the Allies for the punctual payment of reparations, to be able to restore the economy and take the necessary measures to halt the escalating inflation in the value of the mark. The origins of the post-war German inflation went back to the decision in 1914 to increase the circulation of paper money to help pay for the war. Inflation benefited the great industrialists, but destroyed the savings of the self-employed and the middle classes. It also caused great hardship for those who were on a fixed income. Inflation caused whole classes to lose any confidence they might ever have had in the Republic.

▼ At the end of the First World War German battleships were paralysed by the mutiny in the North Sea of November 1918.

The formation of the Nazi party

In November 1918 Adolf Hitler was an unknown Lance Corporal with a good war record. Before 1914 he had been a loner, who could not settle down to the tedium of a regular job. He drifted around Vienna and Munich picking up the extreme racist and nationalist views that were popular at that date. In the army he found for the first time a sense of purpose and comradeship. Later he described how the news of the revolution reached him while he was in hospital recovering from the effects of a British gas attack:

Everything went black before my eyes; I tottered and groped my way back to the dormitory, threw myself on my bunk and dug my burning head into my blanket and pillow.[1]

Hitler soon became convinced that fate had chosen him to save Germany. When he returned to his regiment in Munich in December 1918, he found a city in revolutionary turmoil. Order was only restored by

Adolf Hitler at the height of his powers as Führer and Chancellor of the German Reich in 1936. In 1920 he was just an obscure rabble rouser, unknown outside Munich.

the Freikorps in May 1919. The army authorities exploited Hitler's fanaticism to use him as an agent to counter the spread of communist propaganda amongst the troops. He attended meetings of the German Workers' Party, one of the many small nationalist and anti-semitic groups that sprang up in Germany after 1918 in reaction to defeat and revolution. Hitler was so impressed by it that he became a full-time member.

He soon became its most dynamic member. He helped draw up its 25-point programme, the key points of which were:

1. We demand the union of all Germans in a Greater Germany . . .
2. We demand . . . the revocation of the peace treaties of Versailles and Saint Germain.
3. We demand land and territory to feed our people and to settle our surplus population.
4. Only members of the nation may be citizens of the state. Only those of German

Spartakists (communists) take cover behind a barricade of papers and newspaper bales during a street battle in Berlin in January 1919. Their attempts to gain power were crushed by government troops.

blood, whatever their creed, may be members of the nation. Accordingly no Jew may be a member of the nation.
5. All citizens shall have equal rights.[2]

The party soon changed its name to the National Socialist Workers' Party (or Nazi for short), so that it could attract both socialists and nationalists. Hitler organized its propaganda, and was its most effective public speaker. Thanks to his contacts with the army Hitler raised money to buy a newspaper for the party and set up the S.A., which protected Nazi rallies from being broken up by communists. In July 1921 Hitler was strong enough to take over the party leadership himself, and by 1922 the party was one of the leading nationalist groups in Bavaria.

The Ruhr Crisis and the Munich Putsch

In 1923 Hitler's chance seemed to have come. The French occupied the Ruhr in January in response to German delays in paying reparations. The German government responded by encouraging a policy of passive resistance amongst the workers, which was financed by printing even more paper money. This inevitably led to uncontrollable hyper-inflation. At first public opinion supported the government, but in September the new Chancellor, Gustav Stresemann, was forced by the collapse of the mark to negotiate with the French. This led to a revival of unrest in Germany. Communist revolts were prevented in Saxony and Thuringia, by the government sending in troops and using emergency powers under Article 48 of the Weimar Constitution to restore order.

In Munich Hitler played a key part in setting up a coalition of the extreme nationalist groups in Bavaria. His plans for a victorious march to Berlin, where he believed that he

In January 1923 French troops occupied the Ruhr, Germany's leading mining region.

could bring about the collapse of the government, could work only if he won the backing of the authorities in Munich.

At first this seemed possible as both the State Commissioner, von Kahr, and the head of the local garrison, General von Lossow, were convinced that the Republican government in Berlin was about to collapse, but they changed their minds once Stresemann restored order in Thuringia and Saxony. This provoked Hitler into staging the notorious Beer Hall Putsch of 8 November. He surrounded the *Bürgerbräukeller* with 600 of his S.A. where Kahr and Lossow were addressing a public meeting. He proclaimed a national government and forced them into supporting it. Unwisely Hitler then let them go, only to find that on the following day they ordered the police to bar his march into Munich.

▼ Stacks of fifty and twenty-million mark notes, each worth only a fraction of a pfennig (penny), waiting to be paid out as wages in 1923.

▲ The accused in the Hitler–Putsch trial, 1924. Hitler, looking defiant, is standing between Röhm and General Ludendorff.

Sixteen Nazis were killed and three days later Hitler was arrested.

With several other Nazis Hitler was tried for high treason, but he was able to use the publicity given to him by the media to turn the trial into a propaganda victory for National Socialism. Hitler told the judges:

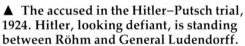

> . . . it is not you who pronounce judgement upon us, it is the eternal Court of History . . . That the best for their people and their fatherland, who wished to fight and die. You may pronounce us guilty . . . but the Goddess who presides over the eternal Court of History . . . acquits us.[3]

After such an appeal it is not surprising that the judges, who had no love for the Republic, only sentenced Hitler to the minimum period of five years imprisonment.

Hitler re-builds the party 1924–9

Hitler was released in December 1924. He found his party banned and its members deeply divided. The political situation was also unfavourable for him. The mark had been stabilized, and the adoption of the Dawes Plan by the Allies and Germany led not only to a French evacuation of the Ruhr, but also introduced a more practical scheme for reparation payments. The German economy with the help of foreign loans, particularly from the USA, began to recover.

How then could Hitler rebuild his party and adapt to the new situation? His priority was to keep control over his own party. He was not going to join any more alliances, as he did in 1923, unless he was unquestionably the leader. He also decided to work within the constitution by campaigning for Reichstag seats until such a time as he could legally create a dictatorship by forming an elected government. He had first of all to re-unite the party, which was split between those who wanted to see the Nazi party become more socialist with greater appeal for the workers, and those who supported Hitler's more nationalistic approach. The party was re-founded in 1925 and within a year Hitler had re-established his control over it by building up his image as the all-knowing, all-powerful Führer. In 1928, for

This Nazi election poster calls on the voters to destroy 'the World Enemy' – Jewish High Finance – by voting Nazi.

> [He possesses] an uncanny intuition, which infallibly diagnoses the ills from which his audience is suffering . . . [He] enters a hall. He sniffs the air. Suddenly he bursts forth. His words go like an arrow to their target; he touches each private wound on the raw, liberating the mass unconscious . . . telling it what it most wants to hear.[8]

Why do you think this made Hitler an effective politician? This clever exploitation of discontent is, however, only half the answer. Hitler also united these different groups by appealing to their common German nationalism. The Nazis stressed that they were a classless nationalist party, which would help all Germans recover their self-respect. One upper-middle-class woman in Hamburg wrote in her diary:

> Every person who thinks and feels as a German, the bourgeois, the farmer, the prince and the intelligentsia, stands by Hitler. It is the nationalist movement.[9]

But the Nazis were unable to win much support from those groups that already had their own organizations and traditions. They failed to win over the Catholic regions of southern and western Germany or the great mass of the working class, which was unionized and voted either for the SPD or the KPD.

▼ Hitler addressing the Reichstag on 17 May 1933. Goering presides and the Nazi deputies give him the Nazi salute. Hitler has just given his famous "peace speech", in which he claimed that Germany was the only country to have disarmed itself completely.

▲ A 1933 poster claiming massive support for Hitler. The slogan runs: "Yes, Führer, we will follow you". It conveniently ignores the fact that only 43.9 per cent of the German population voted for him.

Could Hitler have been stopped?

We have seen that Hitler had built up a party that was able to exploit the crisis created by the depression. His plan was to gain power legally, but how easy was it for the Nazis to win an outright majority in free elections? Commenting on the seemingly spectacular Nazi gains of July 1932, the British Ambassador in Berlin remarked:

> *Hitler seems now to have exhausted his reserves. He has swallowed up the small bourgeois parties of the Middle and the Right, and there is no indication that he will be able to effect a breach in the Centre, Communist, and Socialist parties.* [10]

Look at the table on page 13. Would you agree with such an assessment of Hitler's position in July 1932? When Hitler failed to become Chancellor after the July 1932 elections, opposition to his policy of legality from the S.A. threatened to split the Nazi movement wide open. In August after Hindenburg had vetoed a Hitler government, Goebbels noted:

> *The S.A. leaders assemble at the Command of the Chief of Staff. The Führer and he give them a fairly full outline of events. Their task is the most difficult of all. Who knows if their units will be able to hold together? Nothing is harder than to tell a troop with victory already in their grasp that their assignment has come to nothing!* [11]

Why did the S.A. think 'victory was already in their grasp'?

A German cartoon of 1932 showing the Communists, the Nazis, the Roman Catholic Church and the Socialists lining up to fight both the Weimar Republic and each other. Had either the Catholics or the Communists co-operated more closely with the Socialists Hitler's rise to power might have been blocked.

the army and the Catholic Church were still free from Nazi control. Hitler set up a Lutheran *Reichskirche* with a pro-Nazi priest as a bishop. The political parties, the trade unions and the local state governments were either dissolved or brought under Nazi control by the process known as *Gleichschaltung*.

In 1934 Hitler strengthened his position still further. In a dramatic purge he removed many of his old critics from both inside and outside his own party who were showing too much independence. In the 'Night of the Long Knives' on 30 June, Röhm and the main S.A. leaders, as well as Schleicher,

Gregor Strasser and many others, were murdered. Von Papen himself only narrowly missed assassination and was hurried out of Germany as Ambassador to Vienna.

Hitler was thus free on the day Hindenburg died (2 August) to combine the offices of Chancellor and President and to become the Führer of Germany. Even the army no longer maintained its original aloofness and took the oath of loyalty to Hitler in gratitude for the elimination of the S.A.

Needless to say, by 1937 there was no question of Hitler giving up his dictatorial powers!

The Reichstag (German Parliament) building burning on 27 February 1933 after being sabotaged by the Nazis. The destruction of the Reichstag, which was blamed on the communists, marked the end of the Weimar Republic.

The Enabling Law

Von Papen was so confident that he had effectively harnessed the Nazis to a nationalist government that he boasted:

> *What do you want? I have Hindenburg's confidence. Within two months, we will have pushed Hitler so far into a corner that he'll squeak.* [14]

What went wrong? How did Hitler slip the leash? Von Papen partly answered this question later:

> *My own fundamental error was to underrate the dynamic power which had awakened the national and social instincts of the masses.* [15]

This painting by the Mexican Diego Rivera, done in 1933, shows Hitler as the master of a culture based on violence.

On 2 August 1934, the leaders of the armed forces of the Reich swore allegiance to Hitler. Throughout Germany troops were paraded to take similar oaths of loyalty.

Many Germans welcomed Hitler's appointment. To those frightened and depressed by the last three years he seemed to be a saviour, who could unite the country. This feeling comes across in the diary of Frau Solmitz, who was a Nationalist rather than a Nazi:

> *Torchlight procession of National Socialists and Stahlhelm! A wonderfully elevating experience for us all. Goering says the day of Hitler's and the nationalist Cabinet's appointment was something like 1914, and this too was something like 1914.*[16]

Why does Frau Solmitz compare this mood to that of 1914?

Those who did not approve of this type of unity were submitted to a campaign of terror from the S.A. which, after the Reichstag fire and the election, at times seemed to be out of control and to threaten Hitler's image of the 'legal revolution'. It was, however, important to maintain this image because it confused Hitler's opponents and won the toleration of important groups in Germany like the army and the industrialists. It was, therefore, vital for the Reichstag to pass the Enabling Law. Why did the non-Nazi parties not refuse Hitler the necessary two-thirds majority? The Centre Party was persuaded by promises of concessions to the Catholic Church, and the communists were already in prison. The SPD was ruthlessly subjected to pressure. One deputy later described the scene:

> *When we Social Democrats had taken our seats . . . S.A and S.S. men lined up at the exits and along the walls in a semicircle.*[17]

Nevertheless they had the courage to vote against the Law, but Hitler still achieved his two-thirds majority by 444 votes to 94.

Hitler consolidates his position

Even though Hitler now had won full dictatorial powers for four years, in April 1933 there were still powerful groups that could have stopped him. The trade unions that had defeated the right-wing Kapp Putsch in 1920 were intact, as was the army, the presidency and the political parties. How then was Hitler able to destroy every rival centre of power within the state except for the army and the presidency by the autumn of 1933? His success was not due just to terror but also to the spell he continued to weave over Germany. His propaganda, speeches and appeals for unity, which could be heard by millions over the radio, gave the impression of an irresistible revolution, which in spite of some outbursts of S.A. brutality, was basically a positive force leading to the revival

▲ Hitler's dramatic style of speaking was one of his greatest strengths and gave him an extraordinary power over the majority of Germans.

▼ The massive scale and impressive pageantry of Nazi rallies were shows of strength intended to impress both Germany and the world.

Hitler speaks to assembled masses in Vienna 1938. How did he manage to rise from poverty and obscurity to such a position of power?

of Germany. On 1 May, for instance, a day before the trade unions were abolished, Hitler preached national unity at a rally in Berlin:

> *We want to be active, to work and make brotherly peace with one another, to struggle together, so that some day the hour will come when we can step before Him [God] . . . [and say]: 'Lord, You see we have changed . . . the German nation has once more grown strong in spirit, strong in will . . . now bless our struggle.*[18]

How would you have reacted to this speech if you had been a German worker in May 1933?

Hitler's charisma was not the only reason for his success. His potential opposition was divided and over optimistic about its chances of surviving a Hitler government. The Nationalist Party, the industrialists, the army, the Catholic Church and even the trade unions, demoralized by high unemployment and by the intimidation of their leaders, thought at first that they could appease the Nazis and maintain their independence. Hitler was also careful not to unite his enemies by allowing revolution to go too far too fast. He did not want Röhm's plans for a new peoples' army and the ideas of the Party's economic sections for breaking up the big chainstores and industrial trusts to frighten the generals and industrialists into opposition or to damage plans for rearmament. A week before all the non-Nazi parties were abolished Hitler called a meeting of his Reich governors and told them:

> *The revolution is not a permanent state of affairs, and it must not be allowed to develop into such a state. The stream of revolution must be guided into the safe channel of evolution . . . We must therefore not dismiss a businessman if he is a good businessman, even if he is not yet a National Socialist . . .*[19]

Whom would Hitler have disappointed by such a statement? As long as Hitler kept saying this, the generals, the Nationalists and industrialists would not consider it worth their while to work for his overthrow.

The Röhm affair, 1934

By the autumn of 1933 Hitler appeared to be securely in power. Why then did he face a real crisis in 1934, which could have destroyed his regime? His refusal to support Röhm's plans for turning the S.A. into a revolutionary peoples' army caused much resentment amongst party veterans and S.A. leaders. Röhm for instance openly complained:

> *Adolf is a swine. He will give us all away. He only associates with the reactionaries now . . . Getting matey with the East Prussian generals . . . we've got to produce something new, don't you see? A new discipline. A new principle of organization. The generals are a lot of old fogeys. They never had a new idea . . . I'm the nucleus of the new army, don't you see that? Don't you understand that what's coming must be new, fresh and unused?*[20]

Why does Röhm call Hitler 'a swine'?

A clash between Hitler and Röhm was therefore likely, but the situation was further complicated by the growing impatience of the generals with Hitler's failure to discipline Röhm quickly. They feared that Röhm would push Hitler into a second revolution, more inclined towards the socialists, that would finally sweep them away. As Hindenburg was dying by the summer of 1934, there was a real possibility that all the remaining non-Nazi forces might insist on the restoration of the monarchy and that would block Hitler's plans for combining the presidency with the chancellorship.

A cartoon in the *Evening Standard* after the Night of the Long Knives, showing Hitler, Goering (dressed as a Wagnerian hero) and a timid Goebbels, supported by the army, threaten the S.A. To them Röhm was a threat which had to be eliminated.

Goering, Röhm and Hitler (left to right), shown together when all three were still close colleagues.

On 17 June von Papen warned Hitler:

Have we gone through the anti-Marxist revolution in order to carry out a Marxist programme? . . . Would the German people be the better for it, except perhaps those who scent booty in such a pillaging raid? . . . At some time the movement must come to a stop and a solid social structure arise . . . Germany must not embark on an adventure without a known destination, nobody knowing where it will end. History has its own clock. It is not necessary continually to urge it on.[21]

What is von Papen in fact asking Hitler to do?

The removal of Röhm had become unavoidable, but Hitler also took the precaution of eliminating in the 'Night of the Long Knives' perhaps as many as 400 of his critics from outside the S.A. On Hindenburg's death Hitler could become, without any opposition, the Führer of the German Reich. The army appeared to have saved itself from Röhm and in gratitude swore allegiance to Hitler:

Unconditional obedience to the Führer of the German Reich and people, Adolf Hitler, the Supreme Commander of the Wehrmacht . . .[22]

How Nazi Germany was governed

ALTHOUGH NAZI PROPAGANDA created the impression of an efficient state, behind the scenes the administration of Germany was chaotic. Hitler governed Germany through a policy of divide and rule. In 1933 he kept on the civil service, the existing ministries and the local government officials, but they were usually duplicated by Nazi officials and specially created Nazi policy groups. The result was rivalry and contradictory decisions.

The main role of the Nazi Party, which was supposed to be an élite of only about ten per cent of the population, was to control and brainwash the Germans. This was done indirectly through such organizations as the Hitler Youth and the German Labour Front, which were controlled by the party. There was also an effective system of 'block leaders', who reported back regularly to their local party bosses on the people in their flats, street or villages. One German later recalled:

> *It was considerably more difficult to keep a secret from one's often harmless block leader, who was obliged to report all his observations, than to mislead the Gestapo.*[23]

Why do you think a block leader would be able to gather so much information?

The Nazi party was split from top to bottom by internal rivalries. The Nazi leaders fought for Hitler's attention, and the Gauleiters competed against each other, as if they were medieval barons trying to enlarge their lands. Why then did Nazi Germany not collapse from its own contradictions?

The answer lies partly in the fact that Hitler allowed the experts in the civil service, army and industry to continue their work. Hitler's power was underpinned by the much feared Gestapo, and by the S.S., both of which were controlled by Himmler. In July 1934 the S.S. was made independent of the S.A., and from then on became a Nazi élite force. Its notorious Death's Head units policed the concentration camps and the *Waffen S.S.* became the fighting arm of the organization, which in time was to be a greater threat to the generals than ever the S.A. had been.

Stormtroopers enrolled as auxiliary policemen round up political opponents to Hitler. The S.A. (or Brownshirts) were the Nazi Party's original bodyguards. The much-feared S.A. and S.S. underpinned Hitler's hold on Germany.

In the final analysis it was Hitler himself who kept Nazi Germany together. Only he as Führer could make peace between the rival Nazi groups. The Nazi propaganda machine also made sure that his all-powerful image reached every citizen in the Reich. In November 1939 a Nazi district leader in Wiesbaden observed that:

> *His [Hitler's] person forms the main link between the Party and the people. One has to recognize that we have a long way to go before the Party as such is firmly rooted in the people.*[24]

What is meant by Hitler being the 'main link between the Party and the people'?

▶ **A propaganda poster for the S.A., showing an S.A. man striding past cheering youths and turning his back on capitalism and the Church.**

▼ **Units of the Hitler Youth on parade at a summer holiday camp in 1934. Boys were taught sport, war games and Nazi ideology.**

The Jews

To many Germans of Hitler's generation the Jews, who formed about one per cent of the population, seemed to be destroying all the old traditional values of Germany. Jews seemed to be either great industrialists destroying small businessmen, or communists planning revolution, or intellectuals challenging all that was old and sacred. They had indeed gone into politics, business, university teaching and journalism because up to 1918 they were banned from the top posts in the civil service, the officer corps and the judiciary.

It was easy to blame them for everything that had gone wrong since 1914. They became a scapegoat for Germany's misfortunes. Hitler shared this view, and hated the Jews with an intensity that few Germans could rival. His frequently declared aim was 'to rescue Germany from the Jew who is ruining our country'.[25] However, although many Germans were hostile to Jews, it did not necessarily mean they would condone their murder.

Given Hitler's view, why did the Holocaust not take place until the war? Jewish shops were attacked in 1933, but the threat of an international trade boycott soon persuaded Hitler temporarily to tolerate Jewish businesses in the interests of the wider German economy, although Jews were expelled from the civil service, banned from higher education and the media. In 1935, in response to pressure from the party, Hitler introduced the Nuremberg Laws, depriving the Jews of their German citizenship and banning marriage with gentiles.

By 1938 the German economy was

A poster advertising the anti-semitic film *The Eternal Jew*. It shows the Jew as a combination of evils: moneylender, Bolshevik and slave-driver.

Two Jewish boys have been called out in front of the class. Behind them on the blackboard is written: "The Jew is our greatest enemy. Beware of the Jew". Incidents such as this regularly occurred in schools throughout the Reich.

stronger, and Austria had been successfully annexed. Hitler could now quicken the pace of his anti-semitic policies without fear of foreign protests. There followed in rapid succession a series of measures aimed at segregating the Jews still further and at taking over their businesses and property.

The murder of Ernst von Rath, the German diplomat, in Paris on 7 November 1938 by a 17-year-old Jewish student provided the excuse for the ferocious night of riots, *die Krystallnacht*, in which Nazi mobs were given a free hand to burn down synagogues and loot Jewish property. In January the S.S. was authorized by Goering to set up a Reich Central Office for Jewish Emigration for those Jews lucky enough to be able to buy exit visas. Hitler made it very clear what would happen to those left behind:

Today I will once more be a prophet: if the international financiers in and outside Europe should succeed in plunging the nations into a world war, then the result will not be bolshevization of the earth and thus the victory of Jewry, but the annihilation of the Jewish race in Europe.[26]

Can you imagine how a Jewish person must have felt in Nazi Germany in early 1939?

Education, youth and culture

The philosophy of Nazism was based on a belief in German racial superiority and in war as an enobling experience for mankind. How then were university and school teachers to reflect this in the classrooms and lecture rooms? Apart from a small number of so-called élite Nazi colleges, the Napolas, and the Adolf Hitler Schools, the school system was unchanged. However, in the syllabuses much more emphasis was placed on P.E., biology, German and history, as these subjects could easily be twisted into giving students a one-sided picture of German racial, and cultural superiority. Can you think of some ways in which this could be done? Nazi ideology was less successful in influencing the sciences and maths, but even here it could often make its views felt. In one school maths textbook, for example,

Propaganda was aimed even at the very young children. This picture is from a primary school reading book published in 1934. It presents the Hitler Youth as fun and innocent.

the following question was set:

> *A modern night bomber can carry 1,800 incendiaries. How long (in kilometres) is the path along which it can distribute these bombs, if it drops a bomb every second at a speed of 250 kilometres per hour?*[27]

In what way are the students being brainwashed here?

Further indoctrination took place in the Hitler Youth, which became compulsory for both sexes in 1939. Boys were taught a mixture of sport, war games and Nazi ideology, while girls learnt domestic-science in the League of German Girls. Biased teaching and the interruption of lessons and homework by Hitler Youth activities led to a decline in pupils' school performances. Commenting on the low standard of recruits for the army, one colonel said:

> Our Youth starts off with perfectly correct principles in the physical sphere of education, but frequently refuses to extend this to the mental sphere . . . Many of the candidates for commissions display a simply inconceivable lack of elementary knowledge.[28]

Why should Nazi education have led to a decline in educational standards?

Like the teachers, artists, writers and architects had to follow the Nazi line. Painters and sculptors concentrated on producing groups of nordic peasants, soldiers or large, unsexy, female Germanic nudes, while architects designed pompous buildings in the Roman imperial style. Modern art was regarded as decadent and removed from public galleries. All debate and experiments were banned, as the following comments in a German paper, *The Simplicissimus*, showed:

> There were times when one went to exhibitions and discussed whether the pictures were rubbish . . . Now there are no more discussions – everything on the walls is art and that is that.[29]

▲ A parade of Hitler Youth in Nuremberg stadium on the annual Nazi Party day, 1933. Such parades mirrored those of the S.S. and the Wehrmacht.

◀ A German recruiting poster, 1944, announcing that seventeen-year-olds were to be called up to serve in the armed services. A halo of light seems to protect the boys from any danger. How easy was it to be caught up by such pictures?

The role of women

Nazi ideology had very definite ideas about the role of women in society. At the Nuremberg rally in 1934 Hitler described it as follows:

> *If one says that man's world is the state, his struggle, his readiness to devote his powers to the service of the community, one might be tempted to say that the world of women is a smaller world. For her world is her husband, her family, her children and her house. But where would the greater world be if there were no one to care for the small world? . . . Providence has entrusted to women the cares of that world which is peculiarly her own . . . Every child that a woman brings into the world is a battle waged for the existence of her people.*[30]

What does this suggest about Hitler's view of the role of women in society?

The Nazi government tried hard to discourage women from working, unless they were helping their husbands on the land. Women were banned from becoming members of the Reichstag or from the higher posts in the legal profession. They were also stopped from serving on juries because they were allegedly unable to 'think logically or reason objectively, since they are ruled only by emotion' (Reported in the *Morning Post*).[31]

In 1933 married women doctors and civil servants were dismissed. The number of girls studying in higher education was also drastically reduced. Only within the Womens' Sections of the party could ambitious Nazi women make a career.

The government tried to persuade women

A factory producing radios for the Ministry of Propaganda. The radio was used by Goebbels for spreading mass propaganda.

In idealizing the German mother the Third Reich relegated women to the kitchen and the pains of childbirth – it was considered a women's duty to produce four children by a racially pure German man in order to maintain the great German Empire the Reich was hoping to establish.

to give up working in the factories and offices by making marriage financially attractive by offering generous loans, maternity grants and family allowances. At first the government had some successes, but surely it was trying to challenge an inevitable trend? Since 1914 women had increasingly begun to move into the workplace in all modern industrial societies.

Not surprisingly the Nazis failed in their campaign to keep women at home. Many employers preferred them to men because they were cheaper. By 1937, when it was already becoming difficult to find workers, industry began to recruit women to work in the new factories set up under the Four Year Plan. The Government found itself forced

to give up its earlier rule that only unemployed women could receive marriage loans.

Nazi propaganda reluctantly accepted women working in industry. A female propagandist wrote in 1940:

> It has always been our chief article of faith that woman's place is in the home – but since the whole of Germany is our home we must serve her wherever we can best do so.[32]

What does she mean by 'the whole of Germany is our home'?

An economic survey 1933–9

HITLER'S IMMEDIATE PRIORITY after he had made his own position safe in March 1933, was to create jobs for the unemployed. More than a billion marks were spent on various job creation projects: canals were dug, housing estates built and a network of new motorways was begun, which provided work for thousands in the building and engineering industries. Money was offered to industry and even to homeowners for extensions and repairs.

All this helped restore business confidence and led to a big expansion in production at a time when the world was beginning to recover from the depression. A further million unemployed young people were drafted into the Labour Service and Emergency Relief Schemes. Rearmament, which created many new jobs, helped Hitler to reduce unemployment almost to nothing by 1939.

Table showing the number of unemployed people in Germany between 1933 and 1939.

Year	January	July
1933	6.042	5.392
1934	3.773	2.426
1935	2.974	1.754
1936	2.520	1.170
1937	1.853	0.563
1938	1.052	0.218
1939	0.302	0.038

(In millions)

Examine the table above. What was the impact of rearmament on unemployment? Would you say that Hitler tackled unemployment successfully?

Krupp's steelworks in the Ruhr, 1934. The increased production of steel was a vital part of Hitler's plan to revitalize industry.

Farmers were helped by the setting up of the Reich Food Estate, a government controlled office, which had the power to fix higher prices for crops so that they could be insulated from the world collapse in food prices. As peasants were seen by Hitler to be 'the bloodstock of the German nation', since their children were tough and made good soldiers, they were protected from bankruptcy by the Hereditary Farm Law of October 1933, and their ownership of their land guaranteed by the state for ever.

As Hitler needed the support of big business and industry for rearmament, little help was given to the small shopkeeper or craftsman. Schacht, the Economics Minister and President of the Reichsbank, was the genius who financed rearmament by persuading the bankers and industrialists to provide much of the money for it. However, Schacht believed that Germany in the long

A work-creation project under way. Dykes were dug to drain marshlands and reclaim the land. Schemes like these reduced unemployment and secured Hitler massive support.

term had to pay for rearmament by increasing her exports. If necessary he was ready to slow down the rearmament programme, if Germany did not export enough.

Hitler disagreed with this and countered by drawing up the Four Year Plan. Its aim was to prepare Germany for war by 1940 by increasing food production and inventing substitutes for oil, rubber and other vital imports. Large plants were built for making rubber and oil substitutes, and an enormous state controlled steel works, named after Hermann Goering, was built. Although production increased greatly, Germany did not become self-sufficient and was not economically ready for total war in 1940.

The workers

If industrial production was not to be threatened by rising wages and strikes, it was vital for the Nazi regime to keep a tight grip on the workers. The trade unions were replaced by the Labour Front in 1933, and Reich Trustees of Labour were put in charge of fixing wages and keeping the factories strike free. As far as possible, the government tried to freeze wages at their low level of 1931–2. However, could Hitler hope to keep the workers under control by these methods?

Potentially the workers formed the strongest block of opposition to the Nazis. Hitler needed to win, at the very least, their toleration. Full employment helped, but he also tried to give them the impression that they were a valued and important group in a Reich where there were no longer class divisions. In a famous speech on Labour Day (1 May) 1937, Hitler claimed:

> *We in Germany have really broken with a world of prejudices . . . I too, am a child of the people; I do not take my line from any castle: I come from the workshop. Neither was I a general. I was simply a soldier, as were millions of others. It is something wonderful that amongst us an unknown from the army of the millions of German people – of workers and of soldiers – could rise to be head of the Reich and of the nation.*[34]

The Labour Front had a special section, called the Beauty of Work, which tried to make factories more humane by putting in

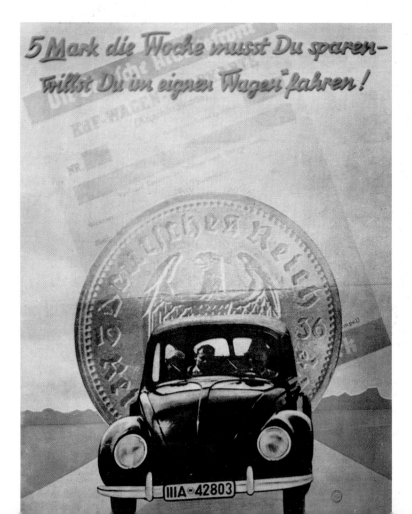

A poster advertising the new Volkswagen. The slogan reads: "You must save 5 Marks a week if you want to drive your own car". The outbreak of war prevented the scheme taking off.

new lighting, improving canteens and building swimming baths for the workers. Another section of the Labour Front organized bargain package holidays for the workers, while plans were drawn up for building a cheap people's car (the Volkswagen) and for a savings system that would help people to pay for it.

How impressed were the workers by all this? It certainly did not stop them from claiming higher wages, once employers were short of labour. On the other hand Hitler's propaganda clearly had some impact. A report from an illegal Social

▼ An advertisement for the Volksempfänger, or people's receiver (radio). The caption says: "All Germany hears the Führer on the Volksempfänger". This was another of the Nazis' effective methods of reaching the workers with propaganda.

▲ One of the Labour Front's posters, advertising the possibilities of travel and holidays for workers – a totally new opportunity for many. This was organized by the "Strength Through Joy" section.

Democratic Party (SPD) underground group in Berlin revealed that:

. . . For a large number of Germans the announcement of the People's Car came as a pleasant surprise . . . This car psychosis [craze] which has been cleverly induced by the Propaganda Ministry, keeps the masses from becoming preoccupied with a depressing situation.[35]

Imagine yourself a worker in Hitler's Germany. Would you be impressed by these measures?

The problems behind rearmament

On 15 March 1938, Hitler staged a two-hour military parade to illustrate the might of Germany's army.

Germany's economic revival was miraculous, but could it last? Hitler wanted to avoid a total war economy with food rationing and no consumer goods available such as radios, private cars, clothes and furniture, because this would remind the Germans of the terrible years of 1916–18. He wanted to produce both 'guns and butter', to keep the Germans happy with his regime. But by trying to achieve this, he ran the risk of causing a major economic crisis and damaging his rearmament programme.

Imports poured into Germany not only because of rearmament but also because millions of workers, who were now earning a regular wage, had more money to spend on consumer goods. Germany was unable to export enough goods to pay for her imports. In 1934 the army began to criticize the Labour Front for not controlling the workers' demands sufficiently. One memorandum sent to Hitler asked:

> *Why is the nation not urged to undergo self-denial and restrictions in order to overcome this economic crisis. The measures of individual leaders of the Labour Front run directly counter to these requirements . . . The Labour Front spends large amounts on buying luxurious houses and similar extravagances.*[36]

Schacht temporarily solved the crisis by the New Plan, which controlled the amount of foreign currency industrialists could spend on imports. He also negotiated new export markets in the Balkans and South America, but by 1935 the situation was as bad as ever.

To make Germany independent of imports, Hitler introduced the Four Year Plan. Examine the table below right showing the actual industrial output of various commodities between 1936 and 1942 and the targeted production. How many commodities met their production target?

▲ A newly-launched fishing boat named after Hitler, April 1933. The plan was to build a whole fleet named after prominent Nazis.

▲ This poster is asking Germans to give money for the construction of Youth Hostels and homes.

Output (in thousands of tonnes)

	1936	1938	1942	Target
Mineral Oil:	1,790	2,340	6,260	13,830
Buna (artificial rubber):	0.7	5	96	120
Aluminium:	98	166	260	273
Hard coal:	158,400	186,186	166,059	213,000

37

Full employment also led to employers illegally increasing skilled workers' wages, which threatened to put inflationary pressures on the economy. Expenditure on consumer goods increased more in the period 1938–9 than in any other period between 1919 and 1940. This meant that, despite the claims of Nazi propaganda, the German economy was in trouble by 1939. Perhaps one solution was a war of conquest, which, if carried out by a victorious Blitzkrieg, would enable the Nazi economy to gain control of foreign armaments production and gold reserves.

Nazi aggrandizement 1933–9

BY 1933 THE ALLIES had evacuated the Rhineland. As a result of the depression, reparations had also been scaled down to almost nothing. So Hitler had considerable freedom of action. In 1933 he withdrew from the League of Nations and in 1934 smashed the French alliance system in eastern Europe by signing a ten-year non-aggression pact with Poland. It was not until the re-introduction of conscription in Germany in 1935, which directly challenged the Treaty of Versailles, that Britain, France and Italy agreed to resist any attempts to use force to break the Versailles peace settlement.

Any chance of united action against Hitler was destroyed, first by Britain's decision to act alone in June 1935 and sign a naval agreement with Germany limiting the German navy to 35 per cent of the Royal Navy, and secondly by Mussolini's conquest of Abyssinia in 1935–6. British public opinion forced its government to take the lead in imposing sanctions on Italy. These did not work, but instead pushed Mussolini into co-operating

▲ Hitler welcomes back German "volunteers" from Spain. Hitler wanted to prolong the fighting in Spain so as to distract Britain and France from his activities in central Europe.

◀ Hitler's main ally was the Italian dictator Mussolini, known as *Il Duce* (the leader). The similarity of their Fascist and Nazi systems drew them together in 1936 to form the 'Axis'.

with Hitler. In March 1936, while Britain and France were distracted by Abyssinia, Hitler was able to break another key clause of the Treaty of Versailles and occupy the demilitarized Rhineland.

The outbreak of the Spanish Civil War in July 1936 made it even more difficult to build up a united front against Nazi Germany. Hitler and Mussolini helped General Franco, while the USSR helped the Republicans. Britain and France kept an uneasy neutrality, fearing the outbreak of a general war in Spain. Hitler was therefore left alone. In March 1938 he annexed Austria without any opposition.

If Hitler had been more patient, Britain and France would almost certainly have been ready to discuss ways of handing over to Germany most of the territory that she had lost at Versailles or in which a large number of German-speaking people lived. This was shown at the Munich Conference in September 1938 where German-speaking Sudetenland was surrendered to Hitler. But Hitler was too impatient and ambitious.

When German troops invaded Bohemia in March 1939, Britain and France guaranteed Poland against a German attack. Then in an amazing about–turn Hitler negotiated a non-aggression pact with the USSR on 23 August 1939. He was now safe from a war on two fronts and could move against Poland, which had flatly refused to return the Danzig Corridor to Germany. German troops attacked on 1 September and on 3 September Britain and France declared war.

1 - Czech territory given to Germany by Munich agreement Sept. 1938 (Sudetenland)
2 - Occupied by Hungary March 1939.
3 - Slovak territory to Hungary Nov. 1938.
4 - Annexed by Germany 1938 (Anschluss).
5 - Czech territory taken by Poland Sept. 1938.
6 - Annexation of Memel March 1939.
7 - Plebiscite to join Germany 1935.
8 - Italian expansion.

This map shows the spread of German and Italian power into central Europe, 1934–1939. Hitler's expansionist policy came first from his nationalistic desire to regain land lost by the Treaty of Versailles, and secondly from ambitions to gain *lebensraum*.

Austria and Czechoslovakia

Historians cannot agree on what the aims of Hitler's foreign policy were. Some argue that Hitler's priority after smashing the Versailles settlement was to defeat the USSR and gain space for expansion in the Ukraine. Others say he wanted to dominate Europe and set up a German world empire. One historian, A.J.P. Taylor, surprised everybody when he argued:

> *In my opinion statesmen are too absorbed by events to follow a preconceived plan. They take one step and the next follows from it.*[38]

In other words he believed Hitler had no particular plan apart from making Germany

9 March 1938, Schussnig, the Austrian Chancellor, announcing plans for a plebiscite in support of "a free and German Austria, an independent and socially-just Austria, a Christian and United Austria".

great again. What then are we to make of the meeting in the Reich Chancellery on 5 November 1937, where Hitler laid down a programme for action?

> *The aim of German policy was to make secure and to preserve the racial Community and to enlarge it. It was therefore a question of space . . .*

The question for Germany was where could she achieve the greatest gain at the lowest cost?

> . . . *Nobody knew today what the situation would be in the years 1943–5. One thing was certain, that we could wait no longer.*[39]

Hitler expected a war against Britain and France by 1945, but was ready to annex Austria and Czechoslovakia in 1938 if there was any chance of success.

Did Hitler plan the events of the next eighteen months? He had long wanted the Anschluss with Austria, but the chance came unexpectedly when the Austrian Chancellor, Schussnig, visited Hitler to discuss halting the activities of the Austrian Nazis. Hitler immediately dictated a harsh agreement that would have made Austria a German satellite. When Schussnig later tried to drop it, Hitler sent in troops and annexed the country, because he could not risk a damaging failure.

Hitler planned his policy towards Czechoslovakia more carefully. Because of its alliance with France he regarded it as a 'French aircraft carrier' in Central Europe. He therefore set 1 October as a deadline for 'smashing' Czechoslovakia. Britain's intervention at Munich forced Hitler to cancel the attack, but new plans were quickly drawn up. Hitler also encouraged the Slovaks to demand independence from the Czechs, so that the unity of Czechoslovakia would be broken. On 14 March 1939 Hitler pushed the Slovaks into breaking away and then occupied the whole of Czechoslovakia.

▼ Neville Chamberlain arrives back on 16 September after his first meeting with Hitler on the Sudeten crisis. Chamberlain believed he could meet German grievances by direct discussions with Hitler.

▼ A *Punch* cartoon of the Munich conference. From left to right: Mussolini, Daladier, Chamberlain and Hitler.

FOUR'S COMPANY

All together. "Well, before we go on, here's to Self-sacrifice!"

The outbreak of war, 1939

Before Hitler could declare war on either the USSR or the Western powers, he needed to know how Poland would react. In January he tried, in vain, to persuade the Poles to agree to the return of Danzig to the Reich. When Britain and France guaranteed Poland against a German attack on 31 March, Hitler immediately ordered preparations for an attack on Poland any time after 1 September 1939. Was he preparing for a general war, or did he believe that Britain and France would climb down? On 23 May he told his generals that:

> *There is . . . no question of sparing Poland, and the decision remains to attack Poland at the first suitable opportunity.*
>
> *We cannot expect a repetition of Czechoslovakia. There will be war. The task is to isolate Poland.*[40]

Low's famous cartoon on the Nazi–Soviet Pact of 23 August 1939. Despite being leaders of enemy regimes Stalin and Hitler somehow managed to come to an agreement, but what did either really hope to gain from it?

He hoped that France and Britain would not fight, but was ready to risk war if they did stand by Poland.

Throughout the summer Hitler put pressure on Poland by demanding the return of Danzig and the Corridor. On 23 August Ribbentrop, the German foreign minister, signed the Nazi-Soviet Pact. In return for being given eastern Poland, the USSR would remain neutral if war broke out between Germany and Poland and her Western Allies. What was the reason for this about–turn? Only three years earlier Hitler had written:

Germany will as always have to be regarded as the focus of the Western World against the attacks of Bolshevism . . . At the moment there are only two countries in Europe which can be regarded as standing firm against Bolshevism – Germany and Italy.[41]

Hitler hoped that news of this pact would isolate Poland. German troops invaded on 1 September, but Hitler was unpleasantly surprised by the British ultimatum that followed two days later, as his interpreter recalled:

There was complete silence, Hitler sat motionless, gazing before him . . . After an interval . . . he turned to Ribbentrop with a savage look, as though implying that his foreign minister had misled him about England's probable reaction. [Next door] . . . Goebbels stood in a corner downcast . . . Everywhere in the room I saw looks of grave concern.[42]

Polish soldiers captured in the early days of the war being marched off by German troops to a prisoner-of-war camp.

War and defeat

UP TO DECEMBER 1941 the German Army won an unbroken series of victories. Poland was easily isolated and defeated in six weeks. Thanks to the Nazi-Soviet Pact the British Naval blockade had little impact on the German economy. So, in the spring of 1940 Hitler was able to launch a lightning attack on France, which forced the French to surrender on 16 June and the British to retreat back across the English Channel. Italy entered the war on the German side in June. Hitler hoped that Britain would now come to terms with Germany. He was surprised by Churchill's determination to fight on, but decided on 31 July 1940 to attack the USSR the following spring. Hitler told his generals that the defeat of the USSR was necessary since Britain was only fighting on in the hope that the USSR would come to her help.

In fact it was his long–term ambition to destroy the USSR. At first he seemed to be successful, but when the Russians halted the Germans near Moscow in December 1941, Hitler realized that he had a long war on his hands. The European war became a world war when Japan attacked the US naval base of Pearl Harbor. To encourage the Japanese Hitler immediately declared war on the USA. He hoped that the USA would be too busy in the Pacific fighting Japan to help Britain in Europe.

At home the production of armaments was increased. Albert Speer set up a Central

Europe at the height of Nazi power, 1942. The sheer scale of Axis triumphs, however, left them over-extended, fighting on too many fronts and defending too many territories at a time when the balance of men and resources were beginning to tip in favour of the Allies.

▼ A cartoon depicting Hitler as a crazed man-eater devouring Europe.

▲ Soviet bombers over Berlin, 1945. Heavy bombing contributed to the break down of German morale.

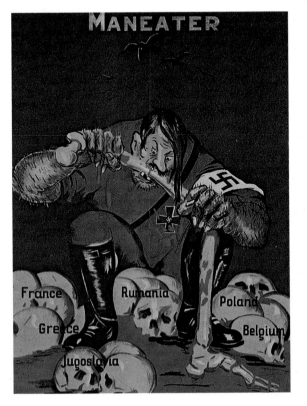

MANEATER

France   Rumania   Poland
Greece   Belgium
Jugoslavia

Planning Board, which was so efficient that the German war economy reached its peak in 1944, despite the Allied bombing campaign. In January 1943 Hitler reluctantly agreed to the conscription of women to work in the factories to replace the men called up to fight. Millions of foreign workers were also forcibly deported from Nazi-occupied Europe to work in Germany.

By 1943 Germany was in retreat. The Afrika Korps had been defeated at El Alamein and, more importantly, the German 6th Army had been destroyed at Stalingrad. By the summer of 1944 the ring was closing: Allied bombers pounded German cities, the USSR reached Warsaw, and Anglo-American forces landed in France. Any separate German peace with the West was impossible because the Allies had agreed to fight on until Germany surrendered unconditionally. Only the occupation of Germany itself in 1945 brought about peace.

The 'final solution'

A boat-load of Jews lucky enough to emigrate from the Third Reich before all escape routes were cut off by the war.

The grip of the Nazi party tightened on Germany during the Second World War as the need for propaganda and supervision of the population became even more important. Party activists argued that the time had come for a real Nazi revolution. Hitler seemed to agree. He personally ordered the euthanasia ('mercy killing') of handicapped Germans. About 80,000 were killed, but public opinion led by Cardinal von Galen, the Bishop of Münster, forced Hitler to stop it.

Why then did Hitler stop euthanasia but not the murder of the Jews? The war changed for the worse the position of Jews in Germany. It cut off their escape and made Hitler independent of any moral or economic pressures from abroad. It also put over six million Jews in occupied Europe at the mercy of the Nazis. Mass deportation of Jews from the Reich to Poland began in the winter of 1939 to 1940.

In preparation for the invasion of the USSR specially trained 'task forces' were formed by the S.S. in April 1941 to execute Jews and communist officials. In July Goering entrusted Heydrich, Himmler's right-hand man, with the task of preparing the 'final solution', as the mass murder of six million Jews was so misleadingly called. Experiments with a lethal cyanide gas, called Zyklon B., took place in a concentration camp at Auschwitz. The final details were worked out at the Wannsee Conference in Berlin on 20 January 1942, where Heydrich reported:

In the process of the final solution, the Jews will be conscripted for labour in the eastern territories . . . Large labour gangs of those fit for work will be formed, with the sexes separated, which will be sent to those areas for road construction, and undoubtedly a large number of them will drop out through natural elimination. The remainder who survive – and they will certainly be those who have the greatest powers of endurance – will have to be dealt with accordingly . . .

In the process of carrying out the final solution, Europe will be combed through from west to east . . .[43]

What is Heydrich in fact saying?

In 1942 the death camps at Auschwitz, Sobibor, Majdanek, Treblinka and elsewhere began their work in earnest. So important was this work to the Nazis that trains taking Jews to the death camps took precedence over army supply trains going up to the front. By 1945 almost six million Jews had been murdered.

▲ The intense suffering and degradation of Russian and Polish Jews in a concentration camp.

▼ Jews on their way to 'resettlement' in Poland in 1940–41. Many probably ended up in concentration camps.

Did a German opposition exist?

When the concentration camps were discovered in 1945, the world asked why the Germans had not done more to overthrow the Nazi regime. Opposition groups had existed, but they were weak and isolated. They operated in a society that accepted Hitler as a man who had restored full employment and national unity. The majority of Germans who opposed Hitler belonged to 'the silent opposition'.[44] That meant that some of the bravest of them hid Jews from the Gestapo – about 5,000 Jews were hidden in private houses in Berlin; others might listen to the BBC or crack anti-Nazi jokes, such as this one:

A Berliner and a Viennese exchange air raid reminiscences. The former says, 'The raid was so heavy that for hours after the all-clear window panes were hurtling down into the street'.
'That's nothing. In Vienna, portraits of the Führer were raining down into the street for days after the raid.'[45]

Should such jokes be taken as serious opposition to the Nazis?

If a German wanted to smash the Nazi regime, what could he or she do? Workers' groups and student opposition were quickly broken up by the Gestapo. The only organizations independent enough to criticize Hitler openly were the Church and army, but neither of these ever came out in total

Former S.S. camp guards carrying dead bodies from trucks to a communal grave under supervision of British troops at Belsen, April 1945.

opposition to the Nazis. Both Protestant and Catholic bishops wanted to protect their churches from persecution, but many individual priests like the Lutheran Dietrich Bonhoeffer or the Catholic Father Alfred Delp showed great courage in their stand against Hitler. Nearly 400 Protestant priests died in Buchenwald concentration camp, as did countless other Germans.

The army had the power to destroy Hitler. In September 1938 a group of high ranking generals drew up a plan to have Hitler arrested and to hold free elections if war were to break out, but Hitler's success at Munich forced them to cancel it. Hitler's brilliant successes of 1939–41 made opposition even more difficult. It was not until 1943 that opposition groups on both the Right and Left united behind a plan drawn up by Colonel Claus von Stauffenberg to assassinate Hitler by planting a bomb in his headquarters. His fellow conspirator General von Tresckow argued that:

> The assassination must be attempted at any cost. Even should it fail . . . we must prove to the world and to future generations that the men of the German Resistance dared to take the decisive step and to hazard their lives upon it. Compared with this object nothing else matters.[46]

Why did von Tresckow think it was so important to carry out this plan? Do you agree with him?

The bomb went off but failed to kill Hitler. The conspirators were arrested and Germany's last chance before defeat to rid itself of the Nazis had passed.

► Goering points out the damage done by Stauffenberg's bomb to the Conference Room in the Führer's Headquarters at Rastenburg, on 20 July 1944. A stenographer was killed outright and three officers later died of wounds. In revenge Hitler had 5,000 people who were involved in the plot executed by April 1945.

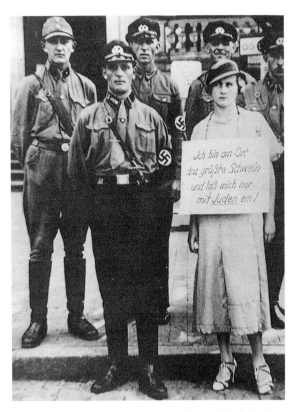

▲ A German woman branded as a friend of the Jews. The placard on her says: "I am the greatest swine in town and only mix with Jews".

The collapse of Nazi Germany

By the autumn of 1944 there was no way in which Germany could win the war. Bombing had cut vital oil supplies and damaged the rail network so seriously that it was almost impossible to keep factories supplied with raw materials. Everywhere there was chaos and destruction. Why did the mass of the German people not do what they did in November 1918: revolt against the continuation of the war? One German writer wrote in despair in his diary:

You, my readers, who will have these lines before your eyes only at some later time, can you grasp it, that such a thing was possible? That our German people in all calmness – Yes in all calmness, that is, without the majority even doing any serious grumbling about it – looked on, while a pack of fools, against whom destiny has long since decided, let the whole wonderful Reich be transformed into one single garbage heap?[47]

The truth was that the Germans had no option. They knew that neither the USSR nor the western Allies would stop until they had occupied the whole country. They also knew that the victors would enforce a peace so harsh that the Treaty of Versailles would seem mild in comparison. Hitler summed up this mood when he told Speer:

Even the worst idiot realizes that his house will never be rebuilt unless we win. For that reason alone, we'll have no revolution this time.[48]

Why did the Germans have so much to fear from an Allied and Russian victory?

In 1945 many cities in Germany were devastated after years of Allied bombing had reduced them to rubble. This picture of the centre of Frankfurt shows the enormity of the damage it suffered.

▲ Field-Marshal Montgomery reads over the surrender pact of the German armed forces in the West, 5 May 1945.

▼ Hitler the warlord. In reality, by 1944 he was a sick and broken man, but he remained in command of the German war machine.

By April 1945 the end had almost come. Hitler shot himself in his bunker in Berlin on 30 April, and on 8 May all the remaining German armed forces surrendered.

Hitler had destroyed the German Reich. The rivalry between the USSR and the USA, which he hoped would lead to a Soviet–American war in time to save the Third Reich, in fact tore Germany apart. As a result of the hostility between the two superpowers two different Germanies were set up in 1949.

What legacy has Hitler left the German people? In the short term he humiliated his country and led the civilized world to regard Germans as barbarians. In the long term, however, the scale of Hitler's defeat enabled the Germans, in West Germany at any rate, to re-build a democracy on foundations that are much firmer than those of 1919. Hitler's defeat destroyed forever the power of the old military conservative establishment that had brought down the Weimar Republic.

Leading figures

Goebbels, Joseph (1897–1945)

His parents were working-class Catholics in the Rhineland. He joined the Nazi party in 1922. He was a skilled agitator and rabble-rouser. In 1929 Hitler appointed him the Party's Reich Propaganda Leader and in 1933 Minister for Public Entertainment and Propaganda. His speech at Munich to the Party leaders on 9 November 1938 gave the signal for the *Krystallnacht* riots. During the period 1939–45 he played a major part in maintaining German morale as Minister of Propaganda. He committed suicide on 1 May 1945.

Goering, Hermann (1893–1946)

He was a brilliant air ace in the First World War. He was elected to the *Reichstag* as a Nazi in 1927. In 1933 he joined Hitler's Cabinet as Prussian Minister of the Interior and played a key role in the seizure of power, January to June 1933, as he controlled the Prussian police force. In 1935 he was appointed Commander-in-Chief of the Air Force and in 1936 put in charge of the Four Year Plan. He played a leading part in Nazi foreign and home policy until the failure of the *Luftwaffe* to stop the Allied bombing of Germany discredited him. He committed suicide in 1946 while awaiting execution at Nuremberg.

Hess, Rudolf (1894–1987)

After fighting in the war he joined the Nazi party in 1920. From 1925–32 he was Hitler's private secretary. In April 1933 he became Deputy *Führer*. He seemed to be completely loyal to Hitler and incapable of independent action. His sudden flight to Britain in 1941 in an eccentric bid for peace was a great surprise. The British imprisoned him. In 1946 he was sentenced to life imprisonment and was kept in Spandau prison in West Berlin until his death.

Heydrich, R. (1904–42)

A former naval officer who joined the Nazis in 1931. He became an S.S. General in 1934 and in 1939 was in charge of the Reich main security office, which included the *Gestapo*, and in 1941 was entrusted by Goering to organize the 'final solution'. He became Deputy Reich Protector of Bohemia and Moravia where he was assassinated on 27 May 1942.

Himmler, Heinrich (1900–45)

He was the son of a teacher and studied agriculture. He was acting propaganda leader of the Nazi party, 1925–30, and in 1929 became head of the 200–strong S.S., which he expanded to 52,000 by 1933. He organized the Nazi Security Service, and by 1936 was in charge of the criminal and political police in Germany. He planned the details of the purge of 30 June 1934, which by weakening the S.A., opened the way for the rise of the S.S. The S.S. became a racial élite with responsibility not only for eliminating the Jews but also for creating German settlements in eastern Europe. As Reich Commissioner he was able to resettle Germans from the Baltic territories in Poland and transport Poles and Jews eastwards. He did more than any other Nazi to carry out 'the final solution'. In 1943 he was appointed Minister of the Interior, and, after the July 1944 plot to kill Hitler discredited the generals, he was made Commander-in-Chief of the Army Group Vistula. After trying unsuccessfully to negotiate peace with the USA, he killed himself after being arrested by the British on 23 May 1945.

Hindenburg, Paul von (1847–1934)

In 1916 he became Supreme Commander of the German armies. In 1925 he was elected President of the Weimar Republic and re-elected in April 1932. On 30 January 1933 he was persuaded by von Papen to appoint Hitler as Chancellor.

Hitler, Adolf (1889–1945)

He was born in Braunau in Austria on 20 April 1889. His father was a 52-year-old customs official and his mother a young peasant girl. He failed to gain a place to study art at the Viennese Academy of Fine Arts. After spending 'five years of misery and woe' in Vienna, he moved to Munich in 1913, and in 1914 enlisted in a Bavarian regiment. He left the army to join the German Workers' Party in 1919, and by 1921 was 'the Führer' of the movement. During his imprisonment in 1924 Hitler dictated *Mein Kampf* to Rudolf Hess. This book became the 'bible' of the Nazis and provided insight into his ideas. It contains his thoughts on political organization and propaganda, shows his hatred and fear of the Jews and outlines his future plans for the destruction of the Versailles Treaty and the colonization of western USSR for German *lebensraum*. It also reveals certain contradictions in Nazi thinking: on the one hand Hitler wanted to return to the 'good old days' before the industrial revolution when there were only farms and small workshops, on the other hand his plans to wage war on France and the USSR meant that the Nazis would need the latest technology in industry and science. In 1933 Hitler led the movement to electoral success. On the death of Hindenburg in August 1934 Hitler became both Führer and Chancellor of the German Reich – positions he held until his death on 30 April 1945.

Ribbentrop, Joachim von (1893–1946)

He was the owner of a wine export firm. He joined the Nazi party in 1932 and became Hitler's adviser on foreign policy. After serving as German Ambassador in Britain, he became foreign minister. He was hanged at Nuremberg in 1946.

Röhm, Ernst (1887–1934)

He was a regular army Captain until 1923 when he was dismissed for his part in the Munich Putsch. After spending two years in Bolivia as a military instructor he took command of the S.A. in 1930 and built it up to a membership of 4½ million by 1933. To Röhm the S.A. was the most important part of the Nazi movement. He therefore felt betrayed by Hitler's support for the existing army. The resulting tension led to the 'Night of the Long Knives'.

Schacht, Hjalmar (1877–1970)

Schacht was appointed Head of the Reichsbank in 1923. He persuaded many bankers and industrialists to support Hitler between 1930 and 1933. He became Minister of Economics in 1934. He then masterminded the financing of German rearmament, but in 1936 he became critical of Hitler's determination to accelerate rearmament even though money was running out. In 1937 he resigned as Minister of Economics and in 1939 was dismissed from the Reichsbank. He was arrested by the Nazis in July 1944 on suspicion of plotting against Hitler, but at Nuremberg he was acquitted by the Allies of crimes against humanity.

Speer, Albert (1905–1981)

He was an architect attracted by Hitler's charisma. He planned the design of Nazi rallies and parades after 1933, and was in charge of the Beauty of Labour department of the Labour Front. In 1942 he became Minister of Armaments and War Production and increased output enormously. At Nuremberg he was the only Nazi to acknowledge the evil of the Nazi regime.

Strasser, Gregor (1892–1934)

He was leader of the more socialistic North German branch of the Nazi party. He was critical of Hitler's links with the industrialists between 1930 and 1932. He wanted to join the Schleicher Cabinet in December 1932 and resigned from the party when Hitler vetoed this. He was murdered by the Nazis on 30 June 1934.

Important dates

1918
9 November   A republic is declared in Berlin.
11 November   The armistice is signed.

1919
28 June   The Treaty of Versailles signed.
16 September   Hitler joins the German Workers' Party.

1920
24 February   The twenty-five points programme of the National Socialist German Workers' Party.

1921
29 July   Hitler elected chairman of the Nazi party.

1923
11 January   French occupy the Ruhr.
8–9 November   The Munich Putsch.

1924
27 March   Hitler sentenced to five years' imprisonment.
23 December   Hitler released from prison.

1925
27 February   The Nazi party re–founded.

1929
29 October   The Wall Street Crash.

1930
30 March   Brüning appointed Chancellor.
14 September   Reichstag election: Nazis win 107 seats.

1932
March–April   Presidential election: Hindenburg re-elected.
30 May   Brüning resigns. Von Papen Chancellor.
31 July   Reichstag election: Nazis win 230 seats.
12 September   Von Papen dissolves the Reichstag.
6 November   Nazis win 196 seats.
2 December   Von Papen resigns and Schleicher appointed Chancellor.

1933
30 January   Schleicher resigns and Hitler appointed Chancellor.
27 February   Reichstag Fire.
5 March   Reichstag election: Nazis win 288 seats.
23 March   Enabling Law.
14 July   Law against the new formation of parties.
        Concordat signed with the Vatican.
29 September   Reich Entailed Farm Law.
October   Germany leaves League of Nations.
26 January   Non-aggression pact with Poland signed.
30 June   'Night of the Long Knives'.
2 August   Hindenburg dies. Hitler becomes Führer of the German people.
September   The New Plan introduced.

1935
16 March   Conscription re-introduced.

11 April	Stresa meeting.
18 June	Anglo–German naval agreement.
15 September	The Nuremberg Laws concerning Jewish Germans.

1936
7 March	Re-occupation of the Rhineland.
17 July	Spanish Civil War begins.
September	The introduction of the Four Year Plan.

1937
5 November	Important conference on foreign policy.
26 November	Schacht resigns as Minister of Economics.

1938
12 February	Hitler – Schussnig meeting.
12 March	Invasion of Austria.
20 May	Hitler plans attack on Czechoslovakia.
September	Sudeten Crisis.
9–10 November	*Krystallnacht*.

1939
March	Destruction of Czechoslovakia.
31 March	British guarantee to Poland.
23 May	Hitler plans attack on Poland.
23 August	Russo–German Non-Aggression Pact.
1 September	Attack on Poland.
3 September	Britain and France declare war.

1940
April	German occupation of Norway.
May–June	Blitzkrieg in France.
10 June	Italy declares war on Britain and France.
31 July	Hitler announces to his generals decision to invade the USSR.
August–September	Battle of Britain.

1941
22 June	German attack on the USSR.
December	German offensive halted outside Moscow.
7 December	Japanese attack on Pearl Harbor.
11 December	German declaration of war on USA.

1942
10 January	Führer – command Armament 1942 (economy switched to total war).
20 January	Wannsee Conference.
July–January (1943)	Battle of Stalingrad.
October	German defeat at El Alamein.

1943
May	Afrika Corps surrendered.
July	41 U-boats sunk in the Atlantic.
	British and Americans invade Sicily.

1944
6 June	D-Day landings.
20 July	The failed plot against Hitler.

1945
7 May	All German forces surrender.

Glossary

Anschluss	The annexation of Austria in 1938.
Anti-Semite	A person who discriminates against or persecutes Jews.
Blitzkrieg	A lightning war.
Bourgeois	Middle class.
Chancellor	The head of the Cabinet in Germany.
Charisma	Intense personal spell by which a leader can attract his or her followers.
Communism	A political and economic theory following the ideas of Karl Marx, who believed in the abolition of all private property and the creation of a classless society.
Constitution	A set of rules and laws according to which a country is governed.
Cosmopolitan	Influenced by ideas from all over the world; not just German.
Dawes Plan	The American scheme devised in 1924 for German reparation payments.
Euthanasia	The act of killing someone painlessly, often to relieve them of an incurable illness.
Extremist	Someone who is radical and uncompromising.
Freikorps	'Freecorps' or volunteer forces recruited to defend Germany in December 1918.
Führer	Leader.
Gauleiter	Regional Nazi party leader.
Gestapo	Secret state police.
Gleichschaltung	Co-ordination or streamlining or putting everything under Nazi control.
Holocaust	The extermination of the European Jews by the Nazis.
Hyper-inflation	An inflation rate that increases so rapidly that a currency becomes valueless.
Incendiary bomb	A bomb that sets off fires when it explodes.
Indoctrination	To force people to accept particular opinions and ideas.
Inflation	The increase in the general level of prices.
Kaiser	Emperor.
KPD	German Communist Party.
Krystallnacht	The anti-Jewish riots of 9–10 November 1938.
Lebensraum	Living space.
Luftwaffe	Airforce.
Mark	The German unit of currency.
Mein Kampf	My Struggle – the title of the book Hitler wrote.
Nationalism	A strong sense of loyalty and devotion to one's country.
Non-unionized	Not a member of a trade union.

Putsch	A revolt or coup.
Reich	The German state (literally, empire).
Reichsbank	National bank.
Reichskirche	National church.
Reichstag	The lower house of the German Parliament from 1871 to 1933.
Reparations	Financial compensation demanded by the victorious Allies from Germany after the First World War.
Republic	A form of government in which power is held by the people or their elected representatives.
Revocation	Cancellation or withdrawal, often of an agreement.
S.A. *(Sturmabteilung)*	Storm or assault troops.
Satellite	A country under the domination of a foreign power.
Scapegoat	Someone who is made to bear the blame for others.
Socialism	An economic theory that believes that the state should own all important means of production and distribution of wealth.
SPD	German Social Democratic Party.
S.S. *(Schutzstaffel)*	Elite guard (protection squad).
Stahlhelm	German First World War veterans' organization.
The Third Reich	Official Nazi name for their regime in Germany. Hitler declared the Third Reich would last for a thousand years, in fact it only lasted twelve – from 1933–45.
Total war	War in which the whole of the country's resources are directed towards the war effort.
Trust	A group of industrialists or traders who organize themselves to defeat competition and to control prices.
Waffen–S.S.	Militarized S.S.
Wall Street Crash	The sudden crash in share values on the New York Stock Exchange on 29 October 1929.
Wehrmacht	The German army.
White collar workers	Non-manual workers – those working in shops or offices.

Further reading

Bessel, R. (Ed.) *Life in the Third Reich*, O.U.P., 1987.
Bullock, A., *Hitler A Study in Tyranny*, Odhams, 1952, (Penguin, 1962).
Craig, G. *Germany, 1866–1945*, O.U.P., 1978.
Fest, J.C. *Hitler*, Weidenfeld & Nicolson, 1974 (Penguin, 1974)
Fest, J.C. *The Face of The Third Reich*, Weidenfeld & Nicolson, 1970 (Penguin, 1979).
Grunberger, R., *A Social History of The Third Reich*, Weidenfeld & Nicolson, 1971 (Penguin, 1971).
Noakes, J. and Pridham, G. (Ed.) *Documents on Nazism 1919–1945*, Cape, 1974.
Noakes, J. and Pridham, G. (Ed.) *Nazism* (2 vols). A Documentary Reader, Exeter Studies in History, nos. 6 & 8, Exeter University, 1983 & 1984.
Prittie, T., *Germans Against Hitler*, Hutchinson, 1964.
Williamson, D.G. *The Third Reich*, Longman, 1982.
Wistrich, R., *Who's Who in Nazi Germany*, Weidenfeld & Nicolson, 1982.

Picture acknowledgements

The author and publishers would like to thank the following for allowing their illustrations to be reproduced in this book: E.T. Archive 5 (top), 15 (left), 31 (left), 39 (left); Popperfoto 23 (bottom); Topham Picture Library cover, 7, 9 (bottom), 11, 13, 15 (right), 16, 17, 19, 20, 22 (top), 23, 25, 28, 29, 31 (right), 33, 37 (left), 39 (right), 40 (left & right), 42, 43 (left & right), 44, 45, 47 (top & bottom), 49 (top), 50, 52, 53 (top & bottom); Wayland Picture Library 6, 24, 27 (bottom), 38, 51 (top); Weimar Archive 5 (bottom), 8, 9 (top), 10, 12, 14, 18, 21, 26, 27 (top), 30, 32, 34, 35, 36, 37 (right), 48, 49 (bottom), 51 (bottom). The maps were supplied by Peter Bull.

Notes on sources

1 D.C. Watt, *Hitler's Mein Kampf*, Hutchinson, London, 1969, p. 185.
2 Ed. J. Noakes & G. Pridham, *Documents on Nazism*, Jonathan Cape, London, 1974, pp. 37–9.
3 Ibid. p.63.
4 G. Craig, *Germany, 1866–1945*, O.U.P. Oxford, 1978, p. 545.
5 K.D. Bracher, *The German Dictatorship*, Penguin, London, 1973, p. 179.
6 Bruno Gebhardt, *Handbuch der Deutschen Geschichte*, Union Verlag, 1959, p. 352.
7 *Ibid*. pp. 346–7.
8 Craig, op. cit. p. 546.
9 Noakes & Pridham, op. cit. p. 110.
10 A. Bullock, *Hitler: A Study in Tyranny*, Penguin, London, 1962, p. 217.
11 Noakes & Pridham, op. cit. p. 136.
12 Ibid. p. 142.
13 Orlow quoted in Williamson, *The Third Reich*, Longman, London, 1982, p. 7.
14 Bracher, op. cit. p. 248.
15 Von Papen, *Memoirs*, André Deutsch, London, p. 256.
16 Noakes & Pridham, op. cit. p. 161.
17 Ibid. p. 193.
18 J.C. Fest, *Hitler*, Penguin, London, 1977, p. 628.
19 Bullock, op. cit. p. 281.
20 Craig, op. cit. p. 588.
21 Bullock, op. cit. p. 299.
22 Ibid. p. 309.
23 Ed. J. Noakes, *Government, Party & People in Nazi Germany*, University of Exeter, 1980, p. 28.
24 Ibid. p. 28.
25 Bullock, op. cit. p. 96.
26 D.G. Williamson, *The Third Reich*, Longman, London, 1982, p. 88.
27 Noakes & Pridham, *Nazism, 1919–1945*, vol.2, (Exeter Studies no. 8), University of Exeter, 1984, p. 439.
28 Grunberger, *A Social History of The Third Reich*, Penguin, London, 1974, p. 371.
29 Ibid. p. 540.
30 Williamson, op. cit. p. 85.
31 Grunberger, p. 331.
32 Ibid. p. 328.
33 Williamson, op. cit. p. 84.
34 Baynes, ed., *Hitler's speeches*, vol.I. 1922–1939, O.U.P., Oxford, 1942 pp. 620–621.
35 Noakes & Pridham, (*Nazism;* vol. II), op. cit. p. 353.
36 Ibid. p. 270.
37 Noakes & Pridham, op. cit. p. 412.
38 A.J.P. Taylor, *The Origins of the Second World War*, Hamish Hamilton, London, 1961, p. 69.
39 Extract from Documents on German Foreign Policy, (D.G.F.P.) 1918–45, Series D (1933–37) vol.I, H.M.S.O., 1950–pp. 29–38.
40 Noakes & Pridham, op. cit. p. 559.
41 Extract from D.G.F.P., Series C., vol. V, no. 490 (6), pp. 854–5.
42 Noakes & Pridham, op. cit. pp. 570–571.
43 Ibid p. 489.
44 H. Rothfels, *The German Opposition to Hitler*, (O. Wolff), London, 1973, p. 28.
45 Grunberger, op. cit. p. 429.
46 Bullock, op. cit. p. 739.
47 Craig, op. cit. p. 761.
48 Ibid. pp. 761–2.

Index

Figures in **bold** refer to illustrations.